Chinese Tunes for
Clarinet

Suitable from beginner up to Grade 2

Piano accompaniment score

FABER *ff* MUSIC

Contents

Please note that the order of the accompaniments varies slightly to the order of the parts booklet.

3

A Happy Moment

Yuan Yuan

Andante

Morning Song

Yuan Yuan

Moderato

4

A Leaf

Yuan Yuan

Allegretto

Four Seasons

Yuan Yuan

Andante

The Creek

Yuan Yuan

Dance

Yuan Yuan

Spring

Moderato

Yuan Yuan

Feathers

Yuan Yuan

Beautiful Garden

Andante grazioso

Yuan Yuan

After School

Yuan Yuan

It's Raining

Yuan Yuan

Cloud

Yuan Yuan

Moderato

Flower Dance

Yuan Yuan

Allegro grazioso

The Shepherd

Allegretto giocoso

Yuan Yuan

Hometown

Moderato

Yuan Yuan

14

Brown Shoes

Yuan Yuan

Happy Summer Days

Yuan Yuan

Memories of Childhood

Yuan Yuan

In the Village

Yuan Yuan

Candy

Yuan Yuan

Going Up the Mountain

Yuan Yuan

Yimeng Mountain Song

Chinese trad. folksong

The Happy Bird

Yuan Yuan

18

Jasmine

Chinese trad. folksong

Travelling West

Chinese trad. folksong

Beautiful Home

The Small River

Baby Elephant Dance

Yuan Yuan

Boyhood

Yuan Yuan

Through the Blue Sky

Yuan Yuan

Moonlight Over Spring River

Chinese trad. classical music

Summer

Yuan Yuan

Busy Market

Yuan Yuan

The Windmill

Yuan Yuan

First published in the UK in 2024 by Faber Music Ltd
Brownlow Yard, 12 Roger Street, London WC1N 2JU
Every effort has been made to trace the copyright holders and obtain permission to reproduce this material.
Please contact Faber Music with any queries.
Compiled by Yuan Yuan and Liu Ruosha
Music engraving by SEL Music Art Ltd
Cover design by Chloë Alexander Design
Printed in England by Caligraving Ltd
All rights reserved

ISBN10: 0-571-54334-0
EAN13: 978-0-571-54334-2

To buy Faber Music publications or to find out about the full range of titles available
please contact your local retailer or Faber Music sales enquiries:

Faber Music Ltd, Burnt Mill, Elizabeth Way, Harlow CM20 2HX England
Tel: +44 (0)1279 82 89 82
fabermusic.com